BARBARIANS:
HOW BABY BOOMERS, IMMIGRANTS, AND ISLAM SCREWED MY GENERATION

BY LAUREN SOUTHERN

Printed in Canada

First Printing, 2016

ISBN-13:978-1541136946
ISBN-10:1541136942

Rebel News Network Ltd.
PO Box 73536, Wychwood PO
Toronto, ON M6C4A7

Cover and book design by Saundra Jones, Torch Agency.

"Lauren Southern is a millennial Ann Coulter. She has the gravitas of Pat Buchanan but conveys a topic like "The Death of the West" in a surprisingly hilarious tone. I read this book in one sitting because it's impossible to put down.

She clearly identifies the problem with her generation. We realize they are more spoiled and fragile than we originally thought and they're on a crash course to extinction. However, Lauren uses this as a springboard to discuss the problems with our entire culture including mass immigration, lack of patriotism, the end of the family, and a slew of other bad habits we've picked up in our quest to virtue signal to others.

They're scary topics and the truth hurts but the answers and hope Lauren provides makes this ominous book incredibly inspiring. She may have cut her teeth doing videos but it's clear she has a bright future as a writer. That's good news, for all of us."

- Gavin McInnes

"*Lauren Southern has written a fiery, passionate, intense and essential book – a bright spinning flashlight thrown down the well of cultural darkness that can truly help those with a thirst to climb their way out of the modern sewage of leftist madness. Modern globalism's sickly, relativistic hedonism – combined with its totalitarian intolerance – has met its match in this angry, funny and powerfully optimistic work. Reading this book is like stumbling upon an oasis in a desert – a haven filled not with water, but whiskey and bullets and gritted teeth. Buy it, read it, share it – if you have no spine, you will surely grow one – and if you have one, prepare to have it stiffened with resolution. You are not alone. Read "Barbarians: How Baby Boomers, Immigrants, and Islam Screwed My Generation," go forth and conquer.*"

- Stefan Molyneux

TABLE OF CONTENTS

ACKNOWLEDGEMENTS

I'd like to thank my father for his wisdom.

Thank you to my brilliant friend, editor, and frequent Skype buddy Mytheos Holt.

Thank you to Ezra Levant for making this book and my career possible.

And to my generation, who despite their many flaws, may yet become the shield to barbarism's death blow, a dagger at the heart of globalism, and a purifying stream that will stop civilization from burning.

INTRODUCTION

Lauren Southern burst onto the scene in a blaze of fury, fighting social justice warriors who had gotten used to conservatives meekly deferring to them. No more of that; whether it was her one-woman counter-protest at a left-wing "slutwalk" or going into the slums of Milwaukee during a Black Lives Matter riot, Lauren dares to say what everybody else thinks.

As a reporter at The Rebel, Lauren has taken on the United Nations in India; the Bilderberg group in Germany; she's investigated the fake refugees at the dangerous "Jungle" refugee camp in Calais, France; she's walked through the terrorist safe-haven of Molenbeek, Belgium. Real reporting that the mainstream media doesn't do, lest their findings interfere with their official narrative.

There's a unifying philosophy behind it. And that's what this book is about: a right wing millennial with a cause. It's a manifesto for an entire generation and a great read.

Ezra Levant, Founder and Rebel Commander
TheRebel.media

1

THE WEST IS DYING

It is the current year.

Right now, you — yes, you — young progressive millennial, can have almost anything you want. The world is your oyster, and there will always be more pearls to plunder.

Is two genders not enough for you? Do you want *more*? Well, Facebook offers 58 genders for your self-identification pleasure.

Is jerking off to porn not enough for you? Do you want *more*? Well, with a few hundred swipes and a few dozen shots, you can get sex with nothing but your iPhone and credit card.

Is our society not inclusive enough for you? Do you want *more*? Well, rejoice, for every day a new petition or Twitter hashtag can give you the high of social consciousness and activism with nothing more than a few keystrokes or a mouse click.

Is it not enough to piss off your parents with loud music? Do you want *more*? Well, congratulations, with the power of social networking and a few well-placed memes, you can join any army of disgraced extremists you want: communists, man-hating feminists, pro-rape activists, hell, literal Nazis! Go to Amazon for your free SS lightning bolt Henna design today!

Is it true? Who cares, if it makes you feel good! Is it real? Who cares; it's edgy! Is it going to make you a better person? Psh, whatever, morality's relative, *man*. The point is there's always more — more, more, more, more, more, *more*! More sex, more drugs, more craziness, more genders, more racial groups, more identities, more extreme ideas, more of everything!

Well, except for a few things. You can sample all of this, but you won't find more *meaning*. You won't find more *belonging*. You won't find more *purpose*. But why should you want that? Those things are downers. Those will make you judge yourself. We've gotten rid of all those inconvenient things, so you never need to feel bad about yourself again. Those are poisonous, evil artifacts of the past, when your civilization was still *racist*, still *sexist*, still *heteronormative*, still *cisgender*, and worst of all, still ... I shudder to type it ... *Western*.

In case my blistering sarcasm wasn't obvious, the above pitch is not meant to encourage you. Rather, it's as clear a summary as I can write of what people my age are taught to celebrate: of the nihilistic, consumerist, *à la carte* political consciousness that has been shoved down our throat to cover up the fact that we have experienced an utter dispossession, dilution, and disintegration of the Western soul. A dispossession that has rendered us incapable of even acknowledging the existence of Western culture, let alone being proud of it, and which has utterly degraded our status as heirs to that culture. Because of this degradation — this willful amnesia toward the West's most awe-inspiring discoveries, its greatest achievements, its most transcendent principles, even its historical identity — people my age are groping in the dark for meaning, and finding it in increasingly insane, fanatical places.

I should know. I was almost duped in the same way: my first warning sign that this was happening was my own educational experience. Like many millennials, I had a conventional modern education, and it's only with a lot of painful hindsight and introspection that I can see how deficient it was.

Let me give you the biggest, and worst examples:

If you asked me in my last year of high school to name five great musicians, I would have probably only got as far as Mozart and Beethoven before drawing a blank.

If you asked me to name five great authors, I'd have mentioned Shakespeare and then groped in vain for anything else.

If you'd asked me to name five great philosophers, I'm ashamed to say I wouldn't even have got as far as Plato.

If you'd asked me about the history of Western civilization, I maybe could have named the Roman Empire, but you couldn't get me to tell you what actually happened while it was around.

The one bright spot, I guess, was that I could name at least a single Saint, and recite a few lines of scripture. But this was because I grew up in a religious home, and had nothing to do with my education.

So having established that I knew none of the things that most sane people agree should be part of *every* child's education, you probably are wondering just what the heck I did know.

Simple: I knew the West was, to quote a certain failed American politician, deplorable and irredeemable.

For example, I couldn't tell you about the history or even the names of the people who'd colonized North America, including my native Canada, but boy could I go on about the native peoples they'd unfairly displaced.

I couldn't tell you about the history of the House of Commons, the House of Representatives, or the House of Lords, but I could've given a lecture on longhouses!

When I talked about World War II, I only really knew about the Holocaust, Japanese internment, and the bombings of Hiroshima and Nagasaki, and was certain that they were all equally bad.

I could interrogate someone else's privilege like a Spanish Inquisitor, but wash my hands of my own like Pontius Pilate.

I knew exactly which side of the classroom I belonged in when the teacher of my social justice class (yes, this is a thing) divided us into "privileged" vs. "underprivileged" categories in twelfth grade.

And perhaps most revealingly, I'd never had to read George Orwell's *1984*. He'd been shelved to make room for a local writer's story of a poor Indian boy by the time I showed up.

I realize now how poisonously deliberate this last omission was. Because in retrospect, what I was really being taught, more than this junk diet of useless knowledge, was a classic instance of what Orwell himself famously described as doublethink. That is, the act of believing two mutually exclusive things at once. In my case, I was being taught to believe that, first, I was special, unique, important, and great beyond words; second, that I was completely equal to everyone, which is to say average and mediocre.

I was taught that diversity is unity. That to regress is to progress. That bullying was Hitler. That George W. Bush was doubleHitler. That British colonizers of Canada were doubleplusHitler. That we have always been at war with Hitler, however defined.

I was taught that war, when conducted by communists, terrorists, and agitators, is peace. That freedom, when exercised by white cishet men, is slavery. And most horribly of all, that ignorance is strength.

My progressive educators, and those who indoctrinated so many like me, have been pulling this con for decades. But I think now, there's a real chance that their racket might fail, because the fact is that they've miscalculated.

They've forgotten that the problem with doublethink is that it only works on people who *don't* think. That's not me, and I don't think it's the vast majority of my generation. As soon as I faced the dismal reality of our current historical situation, I realized I had to educate myself in order to understand why it was happening. At first, correcting my own flawed education and learning what I should've known was like playing catch up with a cheetah. But I think I'm slowly gaining on reality. If the rest of my generation are going to follow suit, they're going to have to reckon with many of the same facts:

They'll have to accept that they're not all that special, and greatness is measured in hard-earned victories, not participation trophies.

They'll have to accept that Western ideals have shaped our cultures into some of the greatest, freest, most generous, most decent, most egalitarian, and most peaceful on Earth.

They'll have to accept that it's not Christian terrorism to push back as hard as possible against Muslim invasion.

They'll have to accept the rights guaranteed by Western ideals exist because our civilization was willing to shed blood in order to shut down its enemies, rather than provide safe spaces to savages.

And, most importantly, they'll have to accept that diversity is not a strength; it's a weakness. Its legacy is not peace and love, but division and hate. It is to civilizations what autoimmune diseases are to the human body. It must be razed, salted, and burned, as the Romans did to the Carthaginians. And no, SJWs, I don't care that the Carthaginians were African.

I kid, but really, this stuff is deadly serious. Because while pride in the West has been ruthlessly suppressed to the point of being forgotten altogether, the unfortunate fact is that it's been done with the consent of those indoctrinated by the new system, very much including many millennials.

In fairness, who can blame them? They've had classically liberal

Western values rooted out systematically from a young age, and the new "progressive" narrative chiseled into their skulls. And that narrative has taught most young people to hate everything that makes Western values and freedoms possible. Rather than look up to giants of history like Charlemagne, Cecil Rhodes, or John Adams, our generation turns to virtue-signaling idiots like Justin Trudeau and Deray McKesson for moral guidance.

This obsession with virtue signaling isn't just pathetic: it's highly ironic, seeing as most of my generation is also absolutely allergic to discussions of virtue. Instead, millennials have been raised to hold hedonism above all. Whatever feels good goes. Freedoms and rights are things for legislators and judges to conjure out of thin air, not precious traditions forged in the crucible of history. Most millennials reject the nuclear family, and the religious values, that our culture was built on because they resemble some sort of "unenlightened" old world of responsibility and duty that millennials want no part in.

In short, squaring the truth about the West with the twisted values they've been brought up to swallow without complaint is not something that will be comfortable for many millennials. But I think that if not now, eventually most of them will take the plunge. Because deep down I think we know that what we've done is not empowering. Abandoning all guidance of our past and embracing hedonism and subjectivity was not some genius idea. Dismissing the guidance built for us over thousands and thousands of years in the form of gender roles, traditional lifestyles, hard work, objectivity, and cultural supremacy was, in fact, painfully stupid.

Because really, what have we got to show for it? Nothing but infinite license to put who and what we want in our bodies, while our freedoms to speak, to think, to dream, and to build get more limited every day. We've decided to fall backwards off the shoulders of giants, and that fall probably feels good, until you realize there's going to be a "splat" at the end.

So with the ground of reality rushing up at them, more and more young people are clawing for anything to stop their feelings of personal, ethical, political, intellectual and artistic failure. And the rotted timber of progressivism is increasingly failing to break their fall. So eventually, they turn elsewhere.

And so, a steadily increasing number of millennials are finally beginning to wake up to the choice we face as a civilization, and to the value they've so long overlooked in traditional standards of morality and beauty. They are wondering: is modern culture really so great if it means we substitute Meghan Trainor for Mozart, Emma Sulkowicz for Da Vinci, or Bell Hooks for Plato? Is it really such a step forward that our civilization, which once shed both blood and ink debating Martin Luther's 95 Theses, is now reduced to considering theses like VICE Magazine's "Dear Straight Guys: It's Time to Start Putting Things In Your Butt?" Is this all there is, or can we do better?

No, it isn't, and yes, we can and must do better. Sure, it'll be hard for us to dig ourselves out of the pit that the left-wing indoctrination and media machines has dug for everyone our age. But it's work worth doing. Because right now, the world is on fire. And while my generation didn't start the fire, with apologies to Billy Joel, I believe we have a chance to contain it, or even put it out.

But first we have to expose the frauds, liars, idiots, and above all, barbarians who threw gas on it. So without further ado, let's get to naming those names.

2

HOW TENURED HIPPIES RUINED EVERYTHING

The first class I ever took in university is probably the greatest example I could ever point to of how universities have been transformed into recruitment camps for Social Justice Stormtroopers. And it all starts with a single professor. For the sake of preserving his anonymity, let's refer to him as Frank Moran.

Frank taught my first-year English class in university. He was an enthusiastic man who had a passion for English, for emotion, and for poetry — at least, if you could call purposefully misspelled, garbled English[1] "poetry."

Unfortunately, as became clear after about three classes, Frank's real passion was just passion for hearing his own voice and rambling on for hours about his feelings. I can't speak for the rest of the class, but I started to feel more like I was paying to observe a deeply troubled human being's therapy sessions, rather than to experience a rigorous academic writing course.

---

1 He was a fan of the work of Bill Bissett, if you want to know why I say this.

Then the first assignment rolled in. We had to write a critical review or analysis of Toni Morrison's Nobel Lecture. I wanted to be an intellectual. I wanted to write the best pieces possible and get amazing grades. I took out all my personal opinions, and wrote an unbiased essay praising Morrison. I got an excellent mark.

As the classes went by it ate away at me, though. Despite the ostensibly academic purpose of the class, Moran started bringing up politics, and with each session, his views got progressively more unhinged and radical.

I tried to keep to myself. Until one day when we had a lecture about the death penalty. At the time my thoughts on the issue differed from Moran. I thought in some rare cases the death penalty was actually justifiable. When I voiced this opinion, Moran glared at me with obvious distaste and continued his lecture. During the course of this, he stated something along the lines of "thinking the death penalty is justifiable is moronic."

It didn't bother me much. The bias was annoying but I packed up my books and left, and in fact worked hard to foster a good relationship with the professor. Everything changed the next class.

We were talking about language, and how language is linked to violence. The entire lecture was about the power of language. Now as much as I had disagreed with the professor before, his statements before were simply his political opinion. This, however, was a lecture he was teaching as fact to the class, on his topic of alleged expertise. It bothered me more than his other lectures because I could not find any factual evidence of language causing bodily harm. It may offend, it may emotionally cripple, it may inspire violence — but language itself is not violent.

I tapped my pen on my desk biting my tongue, until I heard the following fateful sentence:

"I see no difference between the actions of the Nazis in World War Two and using offensive rhetoric."

I couldn't hold my cover anymore. I put my hand up and said loudly "Last class you called those who disagreed with you on the death penalty 'morons,' but I don't think you're an SS officer?"

The man legitimately went into hysterics. He banged his desk and yelled "No no no no no you're a liar!" but I can assure you every single person in that classroom remembered what he said. When he asked them to back him up no one uttered a word.

Every student in that class remembers exactly what happened.

I didn't go to a single lecture after that day, and apparently Moran did an entire class on "the student that shall not be named" the day after. I was livid, and to spite him, I wrote every other essay for the class from an utterly ridiculous religious-right neocon standpoint. To spite me back, he gave me awful grades, and his one last act of postmodern anti-Laurenism was to put this "poem" on the front page of our final exam:

what wud reelee help

is if president bush n his entire

kabinet wer impeechd

4 war crimes konviktid n

all givn life sentences

without chance uv parole

thats what wud reelee help

I burst out laughing. Everyone else stared at me, apparently not seeing the ridiculousness of our exam, or being too afraid to laugh because they were just trying to make it through without facing the wrath of this politically obsessed infant. In the end I passed ... barely ... but the most important thing I took away from this class was not my credit, but a strong understanding of what has infected modern education: the curse of the postmodernist, deconstructionist professors making their long march through the institutions.

And remember that phrase, because it'll come back.

Little did I know at that point how successful they would be in such a short time.

This kind of nonsense is not confined to Toronto, or to some small group of politically extreme incubators for leftism. On campus, this is the mainstream. We can bemoan that, but bemoaning it alone won't solve it. First, we have to know how we got here. Where did men like Professor Moran come from, and how have so many them managed to infiltrate the institutions? Well, it all starts with the worst generation in history.

The baby boomers.

I know, millennials (my generation) are playing a strong game to grab the title, and I'm not letting us off the hook. But in our defense, we've only ever tried to blow up the Pentagon in video games. Boomers tried to do it in real life. Just ask the Weather Underground.

You can tell what was wrong with the Boomers just by their name. The "Baby Boom" refers to the massive explosion of children that came into the world after World War II and the Great Depression. No one can really blame their parents for getting frisky, either: surviving events that traumatic would make anyone proud to be alive, and happy to pass it on.

Unfortunately, the problem with having kids right after all the bad stuff happens is that none of those kids remember it or is grateful to you for surviving it. So when Western Boomers emerged into the world, it was easy for them to take the unprecedented prosperity in which they found themselves for granted. Which, naturally, led to them being absolutely unwilling to absorb the tough-minded values of their parents — values which had made that prosperity possible in the first place. Instead, they wanted to start a new generation of love, of peace, and of no mean authoritative figures. And, obviously, the first people to be overthrown were their professors, with their un-hip traditions and callous logic.

Not that those professors were blameless angels. Frankly, they'd already been eroding the traditional purpose of a university education for a while when the Boomers showed up: a process that began with the emergence of the Soviet Union, when professors reared on the progressive notions of government-by-expertise fell in love with communism, and fell out with religion. Bill Buckley, otherwise known as the first college student to troll his campus, documented this phenomenon in his book "God and Man at Yale." This book so triggered the left of the day that liberal reviewer Frank Ashburn accused it of being the literary equivalent of a Klan rally[2], and Yale Professor McGeorge Bundy called Buckley "a twisted and ignorant young man." And I thought a passive aggressive poem on my final exam was bad...

But insufferably smug, liberal, and moralistic though the academics of Buckley's day were, they still believed in classical Western concepts like rationalism, free speech and free inquiry. In fact, Buckley himself saw this as a point of weakness, since he thought their tolerance for free discussion and inquiry would lead them to excuse immoral worldviews like Nazism and communism in the name of free thought, and thus permit those ideologies — which held no such noble principles — to steamroller them. In other words, Buckley basically thought his professors were cucks, but not full blown Social Justice Warriors.

And he was right. Buckley's day was not the time for fear. That came later.

Speaking of, back to the Boomers. Needless to say, when this mass influx of spoiled brats hit the universities, everything went exactly

---

2   "The book is one which has the glow and appeal of a fiery cross on a hillside at night. There will undoubt-edly be robed figures who gather to it, but the hoods will not be academic. They will cover the face." Quoted in Coulter, Anne. "William F. Buckley RIP, Enfante Terrible." Human Events. February 27, 2008. http://humanevents.com/2008/02/27/william-f-buckley-rip-enfant-terrible/

as Buckley predicted. The genteel, rational academics of Buckley's day saw their authority brutally supplanted by the Boomer campus protestors. In place of the cucked, rationalistic progressivism of the past, those students brought a much more dangerous set of ideas: ideas incubated in a movement that came be known as the New Left. Or, as I call them, Social Justice Warriors Mark 1.

And that's not an exaggeration for the sake of humor. You can literally trace almost everything that makes Social Justice Warriors intolerable today to the New Left. This is because the most fundamental element of New Left thought is a near total rejection of freedom, morality, and of reason in theory, combined with the abuse of all three in practice. To sum this up, consider the words of the infamous modern protester Cora Segal or, as the Internet came to know her, "Trigglypuff." Segal was discovered protesting (which is to say, loudly heckling) a talk at UMass Amherst called "The Triggering" featuring Christina Hoff Sommers, Milo Yiannopoulos, and Steven Crowder. When asked politely to stop disrupting the event with her shrieks of rage, Ms. Segal responded with yet another shriek:

"BUT WHAT ABOUT *MY* FREE SPEECH?!!!"

Unfortunately for Trigglypuff, her protest fell flat. Nobody was under any illusions that Ms. Segal actually cared about free speech, and she proved them right not even 30 seconds later with her infamous shriek of "KEEP YOUR HATE SPEECH OFF THIS CAMPUS KEEP YOUR HATE SPEECH OFF THIS CAMPUS KEEP YOUR HATE SPEECH OFF THIS CAMPUS!"

In those 30 seconds you can see the complete evolution of New

Left thought and action.

It started with relentless campus disruptions by students in the name of free speech and inquiry. The infamous protests at the University of California at Berkeley were even conducted in the name of a "free speech movement," though given how violent, ugly, and childish they got, it would be more accurate to call it the "WHAT ABOUT MY FREE SPEECH" movement. Still, tactics aside, these protests would've been admirable in principle if the New Left had put their money when their mouths were and embraced dissent once they took power in the universities.

Of course, they didn't. Instead, their supposed radical tolerance for free speech turned into bitter and authoritarian suppression of contrary viewpoints. "KEEP YOUR HATE SPEECH OFF THIS CAMPUS," indeed.

This, too, was eminently predictable, considering that the protests themselves had never been anything but cover for communist infiltration — and destruction — of Western centers of learning. Now, this is where I start to hear the angry leftist keyboard warriors: "LOL Lauren Southern thinks Social Justice is a communist conspiracy!!!!" And you know what? I understand their skepticism. Surely, such a charge is completely unprovable. After all, it's not like there were literal letters between communist academics and student activists plotting how to subvert the professions and the academy ...

Oh wait, yes there were. In fact, remember that term I mentioned earlier? "The Long March Through the Institutions?" Well, I didn't make that term up. It was actually coined by German student movement leader Rudi Dutschke.[3] Dutschke's plan, named for an actual military campaign by Mao Tse Tung (charming), was that students should learn all the necessary skills to assume power within the highest professions, including and especially the academy, only to turn around and form a unified leftist bloc once that power had been achieved. Furthermore, they would eradicate the very ideas that would make challenging their worldview possible: particularly ideas like free thought and objective reason.

Needless to say, older communist academics like the Frankfurt School professor Herbert Marcuse loved Dutschke's ideas. In fact, Marcuse later wrote to Dutschke, calling his strategy "the only effective way" to achieve the communist domination required to achieve utopia.[4]

But, of course, this kind of strategy couldn't work without the values that impeded it being weakened, too. So Marcuse rode to the rescue, so to speak, by trying to discredit freedom of speech and thought. Sounding like a less hysterical but still incomprehensible version of your average Tumblrista, Marcuse wrote an essay called "Repressive Tolerance"[5] whose argument[6] will be instantly recognizable to anyone

---

3   See Kimball, Roger. The Long March: How the Cultural Revolution of the 60's Changed America. New York, NY: Encounter Books. 2000.
4   Marcuse, Herbert. Marxism, Revolution, and Utopia: Collected Papers of Herbert Marcuse, Vol. 6. Abingdon-on-Thames: Routledge. 2014. P. 336
5   See: http://www.marcuse.org/herbert/pubs/60spubs/65repressivetolerance.htm
6   "Tolerance is an end in itself. The elimination of violence, and the reduction of suppression to the extent required for protecting man and animals from cruelty and aggression are preconditions for the creation of a humane society. Such a society does not yet exist; progress toward it is perhaps more than before arrested by violence and suppression on a global scale. As deterrents against nuclear war, as police action against subversion, as technical aid in the fight against imperialism and communism, as methods of pacification in neo-colonial massacres, violence and suppression are promulgated, practiced, and defended by democratic and authoritarian governments alike, and the people subjected to these governments are educated to sustain such practices as necessary for the preservation of the status quo. Tolerance is extended to policies, conditions, and modes of behavior which should not be tolerated because they are impeding, if not destroying, the chances of creating an existence without fear and misery."

who's ever crossed paths with Social Justice Warriors. I'll paraphrase it this way:

Absolute tolerance is good. But absolute tolerance can only exist in a leftist utopia. Therefore, to tolerate ideas that hamper the existence of such a communist utopia is actually intolerant, because it stops us from achieving full tolerance! Therefore, we should repress non-leftist ideas in the name of not repressing things.

Yeah, it doesn't make sense to me either.

So there goes free speech. But what about the postmodern attack on reason? Well, to get the grounds for attacking that, you have to travel to France, and look at the work of another group of radical boomer students — the May 1968 student protesters.

I won't bore you with the details of the protests in question, except to say that the main cause of the students involved was a struggle against what they called "technocracy," or rule by the virtuous/ qualified. In practice, this term is sometimes used to defend rule by experts, and in that context, some readers might find the May 1968 protests sympathetic. After all, isn't that what Brexit and the Trump movement were fighting, too?

Yes, but the difference is that the Brexit and Trump movements arose among people who the experts had failed. The May 1968 protests, on the other hand, arose among people who knew they'd be expected to be experts, and didn't wanna, because that would involve actual responsibility.[7]

---

7 For a more sympathetic, but no less damning account, see Feenberg, Andrew and Freedman, Jim. When Poetry

A movement like this should be remembered as yet another example of the French making cosmic jokes of themselves, but unfortunately, we have to take it seriously. Because two of the figures who were inspired by the May 1968 protests would end up turning the cancer started by the likes of Marcuse into weapons-grade plague. Their names are Michel Foucault, also known as the founding thinker of poststructuralism, and Jacques Derrida, also known as the founding thinker of deconstructionism.

Behind these stuffy, academic sounding names lurked madness. In Foucault's case, literally, seeing as his first book — *Madness and Civilization* (1960) — essentially argued that mental health (and, by extension, sanity and reason) was nothing more than a construct designed by society to keep the oppressed down. He would later argue that all of society was organized along the same lines as a prison in *Discipline and Punish* (1975), with the powerful as jailers. I could go on, but suffice to say that if you set out to create an academic rationalization for paranoid schizophrenia, you couldn't do much worse than Foucault.

Not to be outdone, Jacques Derrida ended up creating a rationalization for disorganized schizophrenia — ie, the inability to talk comprehensively. Where Foucault argued that mental health was a social construct, Derrida argued that language itself was a social construct designed by the powerful to keep the oppressed down. Yes, according to Derrida, there should be absolutely nothing wrong with publishing incomprehensible word salad as serious academic analysis,

Ruled the Streets: The French May Events of 1968. Albany, NY: SUNY Press. 2010.

and to prove his point, he made a career out of doing precisely that. And he was taken seriously! In fact, it's thanks to the influence of Derrida and his disciples that Alan Sokal, a professor of physics at NYU, was able to get a paper published in a sophisticated postmodern English journal that declared gravity to be a social construct, even though the paper was an obvious prank.[8] It's also the reason why bots are able to get papers accepted in modern academic journals just by cobbling together random bits of what even the *Chronicle of Higher Education* described as "gobbledygook."[9]

Now, aside from its being really funny, why am I spending so much time on this? Because laughable as these ideas are, they have survived almost unaltered down to the current crop of students, and have done so almost entirely thanks to the influence of the Boomer academics who spread them. When an idiotic Harvard student demands that research be subjected to tests of "academic justice" that forbid "racism, sexism, and heterosexism,"[10] she's just recycling Marcuse. When whales like Cora Segal bemoan the all-powerful, ableist patriarchy between masturbating to SuperWhoLock[11] GIFs on Tumblr, they're just eating the decades old word vomit of Michel Foucault. And when professors like my old nemesis Frank Moran stick illiterate garbage on the cover pages of exams and demand it be called poetry, or spout ill-informed political rants and demand they be treated as scholarship, they're clearly marching in the same insane steps as Jacques Derrida.

---

8   See: http://www.physics.nyu.edu/sokal/weinberg.html

9   Jack Grove. "Robot-Written Peer Reviews." Insider Higher Education. https://www.insidehighered.com/news/2016/09/22/many-academics-are-fooled-robot-written-peer-reviews. Accessed Oct. 25, 2016.

10 Sandra Korn. "The Doctrine of Academic Freedom." Cambridge, MA: The Harvard Crimson. Feb. 18, 2014.

11 Don't ask. Just don't.

Do most millennial SJWS know this? Of course not. Their knowledge of political theory extends only as far as tortured *Harry Potter* metaphors, if that. But they are being unwittingly led by committed, dangerous ideologies who know this nonsensical, dangerous worldview like the back of their hand. Or, to put it less diplomatically, people like Cora Segal are puppets for tenured cultural Marxists, and other malcontented radicals. Even the violent shade of fuchsia running through so much of their hair can't disguise the strings.

I say "tenured radicals," because only in the comfort of an environment insulated from competition by tenure, and from reality by an army of administrators, could these kinds of ideas thrive, because that is the only environment where spoiled brats who once called themselves revolutionaries would never have to grow up. As I said above, young people have done more than our share of damage by running with these ideas, but they aren't the ones who built the dystopian Never-Never-Lands that are the modern university. That responsibility lies at the feet of the Boomers, who drove free inquiry and reason out in the name of chaos, hypocrisy, illiteracy, and madness. In a weird way, I guess they proved Foucault right: on modern universities, the inmates are running the asylum. And ruining everything else.

Well, that is, everything that the Boomer "conservatives" haven't touched.

3

HOW THINK-TANK FOGIES RUINED EVERYTHING

N ear the tail end of the 2016 U.S. presidential election, before the exhilarating triumph of Donald Trump, the allegedly respectable right began telling us that Conservatism Was Dead.

The argument was simple. The institutions of the conservative movement, having failed to stop that *man* — that *creature* — that *vulgarian, populist demagogue* Donald Trump, and no longer popular with their own voters, were headed for obscurity and financial ruin. After all, why would donors keep pouring money into institutions that couldn't even stop a *Literal Hitler* (™) from assuming power in the GOP? Some edgier people even snidely referred to the institutions involved as "Conservatism, Inc" for their over-reliance on corporate money and wealthy donors to subsidize their agenda.

Well, I have some good news and some better news. The good news is that conservatism isn't dead. The better news is that Conservatism, Inc, which is to say Baby Boom conservatism, is definitely dead. It has passed on. It has ceased to be. It has expired and gone to meet its maker. It is an ideology no more. It has run down the curtain and joined the choir invisible (to which it constantly preaches). This is a late ideology.

And you know what? It deserved to die. Not just because its 80's-era solutions were obsolete. Not just because its politicians were uninspiring, scripted drones. Not just because it has devolved into a coalition of spoiled legacy brats trying to be Superman, Christians trying to be Hobbits, and autistic econ majors trying to be John Galt.

No, for a deeper reason than this: because they grew to hate their own future, and the voters who would come to embody it.

If there was a moment in the 2016 U.S. election that epitomized this newfound hate for the young on the right, it was Republican consultant Rick Wilson's infamous, high school-level declaration that Trump supporters were "childless, single losers who masturbate to anime."

Guilty as charged. Well, except I don't masturbate to anime characters. I dress up like them and guys masturbate to me. Not sure if that puts me on the same plane in Wilson's book. Maybe he should ask his son.[12]

Not that Wilson was alone. Later, after Trump clinched the nomination, a particularly sad outfit known as the Buckley Club ran an item titled "The Intellectual Case for Banning Conservative Millennials."[13] Their causes for complaint can be boiled down to

---

12 You know what, on second thought, this is mean. I apologize for pissing on Andrew Wilson. Also, please don't google Rick Wilson Son Piss. The results are even meaner.
13 Kyle Foley. "The Intellectual Case For Banning Conservative Millennials." The Buckley Club. https://thebuck-leyclub.com/the-intellectual-case-for-banning-conservative-millennials-d40d5a7a4a90#.ol8m68oiw. Accessed Oct. 25, 2016.

the fact that conservative millennials enjoy tweaking liberals, being snarky, having fun, and generally not acting like the kind of uptight, over-earnest bowtie addicts the movement previously found so easy to control.

You can imagine how sorry I am.

But now that Donald Trump has actually won the presidency of the United States, forever tying the fate of "conservative" politics in the West to his success, I'd like to make a counter-offer: let's just ban all the people who wanted to prematurely bury conservatism when they stopped being able to control it.

We wouldn't lose all that much, honestly. With rare, rare exceptions, the anti-Trump "conservatives" were out of touch, boring, lame, ineffective, self-righteous losers without enough flare or original thought to headline an accountants' convention. Except, as their reading of the polls showed us, the accountants are better at math.

Funnily enough, some of these "conservatives" seem to recognize how boring and useless they've become. But in their minds, that's a virtue. No, really. Jamie Kirchick, one of the most stridently anti-Trump writers, said exactly this.[14] In his mind, and the mind of those like him, that's what conservatism is *supposed* to be.

I hate to break it to them, but it's not conservatism that's boring. It's just them. For example, while a lot of younger, more iconoclastic, right-wingers like to complain about Bill Buckley, the fact is that Buckley

---

14 See James Kirchick. "Why White Nationalist Thugs Thrill to Trump." New York, NY: National Review. April 11, 2016.

wasn't boring at all. The man jet-setted around the world, wrote a series of successful spy novels along with his political work, hosted glamorous high society parties in New York City with his socialite wife Pat, and might have even smoked weed on his yacht in his old age. Ronald Reagan, meanwhile, spent most of his life as a Hollywood star, married two of them, and had the toast of old Hollywood at his inauguration. And Buckley and Reagan are considered the human incarnations of conservatism by today's dull breed. Conservatives are just naturally boring and staid? Give me a break.

The truth is, the triumph of Trump, Brexit, and similar politicians/movements, is a long-overdue course correction by the political right. Trump and his peers were elected because the right has realized it needs do better by the billions of people who want a counter to left-wing dominance of their cultures, economies, and politics. Honestly, it's embarrassing that it took this long, and contrary to the self-flattery and lies that the old right tells itself, this change did not happen in defiance of principle, or purity, or virtue. It's the opposite: the people who pretend to stand for "conservatism" today have either forgotten or willfully perverted its meaning. They didn't start as conservatives. They aren't conservatives now. And, arguably, they never have been.

This is because, prior to the election of Donald Trump, conservatism was dominated by a class of intellectuals generally identified as "neoconservatives," or "neocons." I'm sure most people *have* heard that word. I'm less sure that the people who have heard it really understand its origins.

The word "neoconservative" is a neologism that started in the early

1970s to describe a class of mostly New York-based intellectuals who had converted to being conservatives due to cultural issues, anticommunism, and perhaps most importantly, opposition to SJW campus protesters.

Yeah. Remember those cucked professors who Bill Buckley made fun of in his book? Well, let's just say they weren't happy with having their comfy academic privileges seized from them by a bunch of vagabond hippies. This group, led by the likes of Irving Kristol, Norman Podhoretz, Daniel Bell, and Midge Decter, were some of the first to defect to the conservative movement, terming themselves "neoconservatives." Irving Kristol even coined a cute little definition for the term: "A neoconservative is a liberal who's been mugged by reality."

But don't be fooled. This definition of "neoconservative" might be cute, but the "neo-" prefix, then as now, should've been the first warning sign: it was basically a way for the people involved to designate themselves as newer and more enlightened than the earlier crop of conservatives. "We're not like *those people*" was the message of the label, with *those people* being pretty much all the people who had given the "conservative" label meaning in the first place. As former ardent supporters of technocratic liberal government, and of the "consensus" that sustained it, they were particularly anxious to distance themselves from people like the supporters of doomed presidential candidate Barry Goldwater — arguably, the original "deplorable" candidate.[15] In other words, they weren't so much

---

15 See Perlstein, Rick. Before the Storm: Barry Goldwater and the Unmaking of the American Consensus. New York: Nation Books. 2009.

interested in converting to the right as in running away from the left, co-opting the right, and remaking it in their image.

And you know what? That's exactly what they did. Very shortly after joining the conservative movement, the neoconservatives started, little by little, to sanitize the right — to make it more like the old left. In other words, they tried to make it more technocratic, more stuffy, more "responsible," less rebellious, less edgy, less young, and above all, less politically incorrect. So, essentially, nothing that "conservative" originally meant. They achieved this by first sidelining, and then outright blacklisting, earlier conservative intellectuals from positions of influence.[16] By the end of the Reagan administration, it was virtually universally understood that, while deviance from the politically correct orthodoxy of the New Left would still be accepted on the right, the right would also have its own orthodoxy, enforced by (who else) the neoconservatives themselves.

Fortunately, this bloodless conquest of the political right did not happen without complaints. A lot of earlier conservatives voiced their displeasure and became, essentially, ideological sleeper cells trying to overthrow their new masters. Far from "liberals mugged by reality," these people saw the neoconservatives as, to paraphrase the writer Stephen Tonsor, town whores who had got religion only to try to dictate the contents of the pastor's sermons. Too bad for Tonsor that at the time he wrote this, the town whore wasn't just telling the preacher what to say: she had virtually covered the interior of conservatism's

---

16 The best example of this blacklisting would be the fight over President Ronald Reagan's nomination of Mel Bradford to be head of the National Endowment for the Humanities. Bradford, like Steve Bannon today, was smeared as a racist and a white supremacist by neoconservatives and liberals alike. Unlike Donald Trump, Reagan caved to these complaints and nominated someone else.

"church" with used condom wrappers and then excommunicated anyone who complained. It would take until the election of Trump for this usurpation to begin to be reversed.

Now, to give the neoconservative "town whores" their due, some of them were very smart, thoughtful people, who brought a lot of intellectual life to the right, at least among their first generation. There also wasn't anything wrong, in principle, with their disagreeing about what the right ought to support. The problem, then as now, was that the neoconservatives preferred to shame their opponents out of respectable society than to debate them: a tendency they learned on the Trotskyist left and never really got over. And actually, even the first generation of neoconservatives could have been salvaged from this: they actually had some degree of modesty about their convictions due to having been so badly disappointed by the left.

But as always, the boomers ruined everything, as became clear when the boomer generation of neoconservatives — many of whom were the first generation's kids — came of age. Unlike their parents, the boomer neocons came of political age primarily during the Reagan years, when their ideas seemed invincibly on the rise. Politically, their parents had been mugged by reality: these kids were practically fellated by it. And that's not even getting into the ease with which so many of them skated into prestigious careers on the strength of their parents' connections and success.

In short, there was literally no reason for these people not to think the Republican Party was their birthright, that their worldview could do no wrong, and that anyone who disagreed was a shameful stain on humanity. Small wonder that the vehicle they would eventually use to cuck the conservative movement entirely was another silver spoon wielding heir to political privilege — George W. Bush. Smaller wonder still that this coddled second generation of neoconservative legacy kids — Bill Kristol (son of Irving), John Podhoretz (son of Norman), and Jonah Goldberg (son of Lucianne), to name a few — would come to form a "who's who" of the most bitter, entitled #NeverTrump pundits. Like W, they went through life skating by on their last names, and were enraged that newer, younger right-wingers weren't impressed.

Well, we aren't. We will never be.

Let's be clear: the modern generation of neoconservatives are deeply dangerous to the right because even in the context of a Trump administration, they still have the means to control how young right-wingers learn the history of their movement, and how they gain employment as professional "conservatives."

Until the rise of Trump, neoconservatives could plausibly act as if *they owned* what counts as conservatism today because they controlled most of the magazines and think tanks that write on behalf of Conservatism, Inc. In fact, most of their institutional control is recent and historically out of step with what the right represents. They ostracize, mock, and blacklist anyone who disagrees with them today, claiming that no one ever has. In fact, multiple great figures in the history of the right have been unimpressed with their worldview, including Bill Buckley himself.[17]

---

17 Buckley: "I think those I know, which is most of them, are bright, informed and idealistic, but that they simply

Nevertheless, they brainwash young conservatives with a historical narrative that purports to show a straight, unbroken line from the ideas of Goldwater, Buckley, and Reagan to the ideas of George W. Bush, Paul Ryan, Marco Rubio, and, for all I know, Evan McMullin. All of this is self-serving hogwash.

And that's not even touching on how neoconservatives have corrupted the religious component of right-wing politics, at least in the States. While most of the people who have been involved with religious politics on the right the longest in the United States (Phyllis Schlafly, Tony Perkins, Jerry Falwell, Jr., and Ralph Reed being good examples) were wise enough to back Donald Trump as a matter of survival, neoconservatives so successfully embedded their own toxic brand of "religious" politics that they were able to hide just how commonsensical such a choice was. They did this through a series of Religious Globalist mouthpieces, who push neoconservative politics from behind the fig leaf of the so-called "Religious Right," but ultimately have no affection for the right at all.

Indeed, so pervasive are the Religious Globalists' sins against the right (and against the credibility of religious politics, period) that it's almost impossible to list them all. A greatest hits will have to do for now:

They have openly expressed leftist-tinged contempt for a nationalist-

---

overrate the reach of U.S. power and influence. Yes, their ambitions in Iraq seem to be leading to their self-destruc-tion." From Solomon, Deborah. "The Way We Live Now, 7/11/04: Questions for William F. Buckley; Conservatively Speaking." The New York Times. July 11, 2004. http://www.nytimes.com/2004/07/11/magazine/way-we-live-now-7-11-04-questions-for-william-f-buckley-conservatively-speaking.html. Emphasis mine.

oriented right, calling it "tribal, cruel, and very dark indeed."[18]

They have openly pushed globalist politics at the global level because it gives them access to a greater pool of converts, and damn the consequences to their own countries[19].

They have whined when right-wing politicians appeal to the pride of voters because "Christianity is a religion of losers."[20]

They have defended assaults on free speech by SJWs because maybe, just maybe those SJWs might let them ban porn.[21]

They have bitched about religious freedom when commonsense anti-Islamic terror measures are proposed, even though those Islamic terrorists would probably bomb them once they got done with the gays and Jews.

I would name names, but I'm pretty sure Erick Erickson, Russell Moore, Ross Douthat, Rod Dreher, and most of the staff of First Things already know who they are.

Let's be clear: the vast majority of religious conservatives didn't sign on for this kind of whining, weak-kneed, Christ-as-Social-Justice-Warrior style politics. Which is yet another reason it's such a relief that the nationalist right came along and made these self-appointed Religious Globalist arbiters of Christian morality pound sand.

---

18 Dreher, Rod. "Trump & the Post-Religious Right." The American Conservative. http://www.theamericanconservative.com/dreher/trump-post-religious-right/. Accessed Dec. 1, 2016.

19 Thomas, Joash. "Why Conservative Christians Must Be 'Globalists.'" Freedom Crossroads. http://freedomcrossroads.com/2016/08/15/why-conservative-christians-must-be-globalists/. Accessed Oct. 27, 2016.

20 Schmitz, Matthew. "Donald Trump, Man of Faith." First Things. https://www.firstthings.com/article/2016/08/donald-trump-man-of-faith. Accessed Oct. 27, 2016.

21 Schmitz, Matthew. "The Case for Banning Pornography." Washington Post. https://www.washingtonpost.com/news/in-theory/wp/2016/05/24/the-case-for-banning-pornography/?utm_term=.c034720b6f50. Accessed Oct. 27, 2016.

They will not be the first. The entire right is now ready to end the dark days of the neoconservative chess club running the right-wing, and of their Religious Globalist allies acting as their Junior Anti-Sex League.[22] The neocons can whine all they want, but the new nationalist right is not willing to keep letting in the dregs of the Third World because the globalists want to fill their pews, or the coffers of their corporate donors. And we're not going to pretend religious freedom or multiculturalism takes primacy over everything if it permits Jihadists to enter our country.

Oh, and speaking of Jihadis and the dregs of the Third World...

---

22 Man, I'm glad I got around to reading 1984.

4

HOW IMMIGRATION IS RUINING EVERYTHING

B efore his father was elected, Donald Trump, Jr., got into a lot of trouble for comparing immigration to a bowl of Skittles. If only a few Skittles in a bowl were poisonous, Trump, Jr., asked, would you still take a handful? This set off a flood of outrage from lefties and cucked "conservatives," who complained that the metaphor was "dehumanizing." Which is another way of saying "too on-point for our feelings to handle."

And yes, the metaphor was on-point. But with all due respect to Trump the younger, I think it was also a bit too flattering. If I had to compare immigration to a bowl of candy, I'd compare them to something entirely different: namely, an infamous diet product known as sugar-free gummy bears, produced by the company Haribo. These candies may be the worst reviewed product on Amazon — so much so, in fact, that numerous respectable publications had to do a story on them to explain the outpouring of bile.

The reason for this seemingly innocuous product's unpopularity is as follows: because they contain no sugar, the candies use a chemical called Maltitol, which is just as sweet, but has a distinct disadvantage: our bodies can't fully digest it. If someone eats only a small quantity of the stuff, this is fine and might lead to mild weight loss. But if eaten in large quantities — say, by people who eat an entire bag of gummy bears — it rots in our stomachs and produces terrible bowel issues. And believe me, that's as clean a description as I can give of the effects of these little gelatinous balls of hate.

This is pretty much the perfect metaphor for immigration. In small numbers, it can be fine, and even improve your country's makeup. But take too many in, and you lose the ability to assimilate them, and everything goes to s—t.

Okay, so that was flippant, but we need a few laughs even when talking about a subject this deadly serious.

But now we do have to get serious. Milton Friedman famously said that you can't have open borders and a welfare state. Even open borders libertarian types agree that this is correct. The problem is that they think you can get rid of the welfare state by having open borders. This demonstrably hasn't worked in the United States, in Europe, or anywhere else. Instead, when prosperous nations with generous welfare states throw open their doors and refuse to enforce their borders, the new populations agitate for more benefits, and sometimes even manage to vote for them thanks to fraud. As these benefits increase, so do the incentives for more poor immigrants to pour across the border, who turn around and vote themselves more goodies, which produces more immigrants, and so on and so on until the entire government goes broke.

And that's assuming the only people who put strain on the welfare system are the floods of new immigrants. In actuality, because the kind of low-skilled immigrants who vote themselves higher benefits also tend to work for lower wages at menial jobs, they also depress wages and take much-needed work in the most vulnerable native communities. As a result, you get two groups inflating the welfare rolls: immigrants using welfare to supplement the deliberately low wages they ask for, and people who can't afford to work for those wages who are now out of work thanks to the government subsidizing their competition. The only people who benefit from this are the elite and corporate interests who make higher profits thanks to the lower wages they pay immigrant labor. Setting aside issues of unfairness, a government simply can't prop up an ever-expanding welfare state with nothing but taxes on corporations and the rich. Not least of all because the corporations and rich people will eventually leave to avoid the taxes!

The takeaway from this is obvious: open borders inevitably lead to the collapse of not just the welfare state, but the whole state, due to over-extended welfare systems. Outside of a few crazy college freshmen, most people who oppose the welfare state don't want to invite anarchy in order to destroy it.

But as you can see, even if you only consider immigration from an economic perspective, an "invite the world" policy still comes out to an invitation for eventual anarchy.

Which brings us to a confusing point — if this is the result of such policy, why would you see it so vehemently defended by both the left and the right?

It's bizarre, but both liberals and conservatives in the West are constantly pushing for more immigration, even when that immigration occurs against the wishes of their people, or against the letter of their own laws. Conservatives' reasons for this are mostly economic. They claim immigration is financially beneficial because it gives us cheaper labor, which improves GDP, which leads to greater freedom for some reason. They focus on the benefits to the demand side of immigration — the employers — rather than the losses to the supply side. Which is ironic, because conservative economics is supposed to be about the supply side. Even more ironic is that the empirical economic claim they make doesn't even necessarily hold water on its own merits. Unless you basically beg the question in constructing a study by assuming the economy will grow the same way immigration advocates say it will, immigration usually comes out to a net negative on the economy.[23]

Still, at least with the conservatives, you can argue economics and facts. Liberals have no such limitations. For them, immigration is all about playing mommy to the poor, vulnerable immigrant populations, who obviously contribute so much to diversity and multiculturalism. I mean, without immigrants where would we have got Chipotle?![24] No one[25] is illegal!

If you *force* liberals to come up with an argument based on

---

23 The work of Harvard economist George Borjas is instructive on this.

24 To be honest, I like Chipotle, too, but I tend to agree with Rowan Atkinson's fictional conservative voter from the 80s: Now that we've got the recipe, is there any need for them to stay?

25 Which is to say, no action undertaken by select groups.

economics or facts, they'll usually rely on the idea that birth rates in the West are so low among native populations that they can't meet the demand for labor. Therefore, we need to import labor from elsewhere. Not a single part of this is correct, or even consistent.

Firstly, if the number of laborers is so low, shouldn't that mean increased wages for those that remain? I thought liberals were all about the little guy! I guess their corporate donors must be okay with the mask slipping here.

Secondly, since when have liberals complained about falling birth rates? Isn't that what their entire platform on issues like abortion, and the sexual revolution, is designed to create? Isn't that the basis for their claim that liberal communities have better child care, better education, and less crime? Because there are fewer unwanted pregnancies? If they really cared about this, they wouldn't endorse ripping babies out of their mothers' wombs at nine months.

Thirdly, given that immigration is a net negative on the economy because it grows the demands of the welfare state, doesn't more immigration equal higher taxes? What kind of sense does it make to endorse a policy that makes native people poorer, and therefore less likely to have their own kids, on the grounds that people aren't having enough kids?

These are questions without good answers, because the reality is that "arguments" like this are half-baked smokescreens for the left to impose its religious attachment to multiculturalism.

And I'm sad to say that multiculturalism was probably spearheaded by Canadians like myself. In 1971, during Pierre Trudeau's reign, Canada was the first country in the world to adopt state multiculturalism as official policy. If you look his son, Canada's current prime minister Justin Trudeau, it should be obvious to you at this point that the worm-eaten apple doesn't fall far from the tree. By now, it should be obvious how cancerous the dedication by both Trudeau's to a "multicultural" state has been throughout the West.

The reality is that none of these arguments hold up. The economic argument is hopelessly optimistic and incomplete. The cultural argument is shallow and backward. The emotional argument is, like most everything motivated by emotion, stupid and ill-considered. In the end the result of mass immigration is the destruction of the economy, of our culture, and of the very moral norms that make those emotional arguments have resonance in the first place.

Unchecked immigration by low-skilled workers attacks the economy from two directions: first, the number of shiftless immigrants grows the welfare state at the expense of the private sector. Second, even those who work hard often siphon money out of our domestic economy and send it back to their own countries, which boosts those countries at our expense.

Unchecked immigration of all kinds attacks the culture because it often allows in critical masses of groups that despise Western culture's most precious heritage: that of freedom, classical republicanism, and the enlightenment.

Unchecked immigration is a moral eyesore. It asks our states to fail their most basic obligations by putting the needs of faceless, dubiously friendly strangers over the needs of the citizens they exist to protect and serve. It is like an airline passenger who insists on putting air masks on everyone else when the plane's oxygen fails. The fact is that such a person has an obligation to help themselves, just like our nations must help ourselves before we have the luxury of compassion for outsiders.

The multicultural worldview that promotes unchecked immigration is not about fulfilling the obligations of a government toward its own people. It is instead a recklessly naïve, utopian view of the world holding hands, loving each other, and singing Kumbaya, even though all of history, social science, and common sense militate against that actually happening. Similarly, multiculturalism is not motivated by a desire for integration or assimilation of the best of foreign cultures into Western culture: rather, it seeks to put every culture in its own ghetto-sized safe space while forcing the surrounding country to conform, rather than the other way round. Instead of a melting pot, it's a bunch of ingredients left to rot separately.

Because of that rot, the ultimate end result of multiculturalism is cultural relativism. And if multiculturalism is a disaster when you institutionalize it, then cultural relativism can get downright apocalyptic. Elites don't experience this reality, because in their safe, homogenous, gated communities, the only form of multiculturalism they see are kindergarten posters of different colored children holding hands around the globe. Judged by this infantile standard, it's easy to see why people can spout inanities like "diversity is our strength."

It is equally understandable, then, why elites react with such visceral horror when their childlike view of multiculturalism is threatened. Witness the freakout by the Canadian mainstream press over an Angus Reid poll showing that 68% of Canadians wanted to see more assimilation from immigrants to Western culture.[26] The journalists whose jimmies were so rustled by this poll must have been spitting up artisanal coffee all over the tasteful furniture in their high-security condos. How could so many Canadians oppose our beautiful multiculturalism? Naturally, the people beleaguered by this racism had to be allowed to respond!

So the Canadian Broadcasting Corporation produced another article, this time purporting to speak for the immigrants.[27] The author's conclusion — and that of the immigrants — was that there was no reasonable explanation for these increased demands for assimilation. It must just be the effects of Trump-style politics nefariously slipping across Canada's southern border![28]

Not only that, but the article even implied that cultural enclaves in Canada were already doing everything they could to assimilate. Take this sentence, for instance: "Lal Khan Malik, the president of the Ahmadiyya Muslim Jama'at Canada, said his group is working hard to build connections in the communities across the country."

They're working so hard to build connections! How could people possibly dislike this!? Well maybe it's because Ahmadiyya Muslim

---

26 Proctor, Jason. "CBC-Angus Reid Institute poll: Canadians want minorities do more to 'fit in.'" CBC News. http://www.cbc.ca/news/canada/british-columbia/poll-canadians-multiculturalism-immigrants-1.3784194. Oct. 3, 2016.

27 Rieti, John. "Muslims in Toronto wonder what needs to change as Canadian poll calls for assimilation." CBC News. http://www.cbc.ca/news/canada/toronto/toronto-immigration-poll-1.3790181. Oct. 4, 2016.

28 Perhaps they should build a wall to prevent this?

Jama'at Canada is the same sect of Islam that applied for a housing grant from the city of Toronto to build an affordable apartment building, upon which they proceeded to refuse applications from would-be tenants if they weren't Muslim. This included Austin Lewis, a young man in a wheelchair who could not find any subsidized housing that could accommodate his disability other than this Muslim housing. He was denied — and it took him three years to find housing after that.

So while these elites turn their chins up at the little people that have to deal with immigrant crime and discrimination, people like Austin Lewis have to live the reality of it. That is a reality that CBC journalists will likely never care to explore or display. They have their narrative and they'll go with it no matter what for fear of becoming "offensive" to the mainstream elites and more importantly their bosses.

Those bosses are, of course, the very elites, politicians, businessmen and "intellectuals" that caused this mess in the first place. The experiment of multiculturalism was thought up in the minds of tenured intellectuals, put on paper by virtue signaling politicians, and then enjoyed by big business globalists. All while high-fiving each other from behind the walls and security crossings of their own gated communities. God forbid they apply the policies of those gated communities to their countries, rather than using them as shields against the consequences of their own naivete.

I asked earlier why do conservatives and liberals keep making up these myths about the benefits of multiculturalism? It's for these men: the ominous "globalists." And no, that word doesn't mean "Jews," and it insults the pain of the millions of working-class Jews that have suffered from multiculturalism for decades to imply that it does.

But it's revealing that I have to make that disclaimer, because globalists get some of the best treatment for their philosophy imaginable. When people are praising it, they never have to worry about its being accepted as a legitimate political philosophy. When people are attacking it, they can always count on the attackers being smeared as conspiracy theorists for even bringing the word "globalist" up. It's extraordinary.

As an example, I actually was taught about globalism and globalists by name in my international relations class as a genuine political philosophy with genuine adherents. But as soon as I brought them up as a dangerous group on the Internet, a bunch of edgy "centrists" snarked at me that they're all a right-wing conspiracy. Hell, even *The New York Times* quoted me in outrage as representing a "far-right conspiracy buoyed by Trump."[29] Tellingly, they never bothered to refute anything I said.

I find it hilarious that according to these people my far-left professor took joy in teaching right-wing conspiracies. Apparently Emmy-award-winning journalists like Lou Dobbs are wearing tinfoil for using the word "globalist" to describe people like the failed Trump saboteur and least sanitary puppet Bill Kristol's hand has ever operated: Evan McMullin.

Apparently despite it being a very well-defined term by the Oxford English dictionary, and apparently despite people literally calling for

---

29 Stack, Liam. "Globalism: A Far-Right Conspiracy Theory Buoyed By Trump." New York Times. Nov. 14, 2016. http://www.nytimes.com/2016/11/15/us/politics/globalism-right-trump.html

it by name in *The New York Times*[30]... the entire word is a massive conspiracy.

Not that I'd complain if these people were right and globalists didn't exist! I really would like to believe no one could be stupid enough to believe in such a philosophy. But unfortunately, people do, including the very political science professors who teach it.

Of course, they say it's harmless. They say it means simply being a "citizen of the world," which sounds great. But behind that contentless phrase are sinister implications. Thus, the more wonky defenders of globalism define it as being "interconnected by removing cultural and legal barriers," or as "the pooling of states' sovereignty into supranational organizations."

In plain English this means that globalists wish to treat every country in the world like an unruly toddler, with international bureaucrats filling the role of daycare instructor. They don't want your vote to count unless the wise men in Brussels, or on Wall Street, or in the UN building, decide to allow it to count.

What do these globalist asshats have to do with immigration, though? I'm glad you asked.

Individualism and unique identity is the antithesis of global government. It's the antithesis of the European Union, of the United Nations, of the World Bank. It causes people to rebel in favor of their own interests rather than those of the elites. Brexit and the election of

---

30 Brooks, David. "Let's Not Do This Again." New York Times. Nov. 8, 2016. http://www.nytimes.com/2016/11/08/opinion/lets-not-do-this-again.html

Donald Trump are[31] all the proof you need to see this.

This is why globalists hold contempt for citizenship, tradition, national culture and religion. These things promote sovereignty of nations — they create unique identities for nations.

Destroying those unique identities is the key to submission.

The first goal of Marxists was to destroy the family and the church because both were foundations for one's life. You could count on both to support you, you could count on them to give you guidance. But for Marxists and their progressive allies, it was essential that government fill both roles: both as your last line of support, and as the people with the power to set the agenda for your life.

Globalism has a similar goal on a larger scale. They don't want the family, the church or your government to set the agenda — they want to set the agenda from super-national organizations.

They want to sweep nationalism, nation states, and national democracy under the rug. They want to leave local communities to pick up the tab for their agenda, and shut out any local voices complaining about the cost. Whether that be financial, criminal, or cultural.

They use the false flag of "diversity" as cover to mold people into how their balance sheets and Econ 101 textbooks see you — as faceless, expendable consumers, deprived of culture, identity or thought.

---

31 Yes, I did edit in a reference to Trump's victory every chance I got, and it was awesome. MAGA!

They've had a strong grip on society for the last decade, but Trump and those like him are monkey wrenches thrown into their machine of deceit. Out of nowhere, Trump and his allies spoke up for those who were disaffected by the failure of immigration and had no compunctions about naming the problem. As Trump himself said in a speech, no longer will we listen to the "false song of globalism."

Which brings us back to mass immigration. Whatever libertarian wonks and naïve evangelical missionaries on the right believe, mass immigration is not about the economy or about moral duty. It's about diversity, and the dilution of what makes our countries recognizable, pure and simple. It's about dividing the people so that politicians and corporate elites have an easier time picking their pocket. As Meat Loaf once wrote, "in the land of the pigs, the butcher is king," and the globalists mean to bring home the bacon.

Though ironically, speaking of bacon, that might get banned if they keep letting one particularly dangerous group in…

5

HOW ISLAM IS RUINING EVERYTHING

U nquestionably one of the most retarded concepts to come out of the radical left in recent years is the concept of "Islamophobia."

I say "most retarded" because, while ideas like Afrocentrism or Affirmative Consent rank above Islamophobia for sheer battiness, Islamophobia does something these two concepts do not do: it puts everyone who believes in it in more danger.

Let's be clear: if the left merely attacked "fear of Islam," this would still be silly, but at least it would be something we could debate. But to brand such a fear as a "phobia" marks it as an *a priori* irrational fear: in essence, a form of bigotry.

That the left should seek to label suspicion of Islam this way isn't surprising. The left is like a blue-haired shark. Or a drug addict. It has to keep moving forward by finding new, increasingly dubious civil rights struggles to attach itself to in order to keep its high of righteous indignation. Having flogged the concept of homophobia for every last drop of moral righteousness, it only makes sense that they would seek to find a new fix. Some turned to fighting transphobia, which is a funny but largely harmless cause. It is probably silly to be *afraid* of Caitlyn Jenner (well, unless she's driving) simply for pretending to be a woman. Laughing at her is another matter entirely, but leave that be.

But being afraid of Islam? That is not a phobia. That is common sense. Even a few of the more honest leftists, such as the late great Christopher Hitchens, and the comedian Bill Maher, get this. Unfortunately, the anti-imperialist left has never been known for its reasonability or its honesty. Anti-imperialist leftists are the ones really animated by a phobia: namely, the paralyzing fear that somewhere, Western citizens might be justified in being suspicious or hostile toward non-Western culture. We cannot excuse their affliction. By giving into it, they have not only thrown their previous causes under the bus, but are arguably discrediting the entire concept of bigotry.

The reason for this is simple: the necessary precondition for bigotry is not cruelty, but untruth. It may be cruel to shoot a wolf charging at your child with its jaws slavering, but it is not bigoted. Wolves are predators. They pose danger to defenseless humans. And as the Dutch politician Geert Wilders has repeatedly stressed, while individual Muslims can no doubt be decent and noble people, just as tame wolves do exist, the fact is that Islam the religion is by its nature dangerous to the West. We can have compassion for people who have never known any other way of thinking, just as we have compassion for cancer patients, without excusing the disease.

Those Muslims we can "cure" of the worst elements of their religion's doctrine, or who seek to cure themselves and their fellow

Muslims, deserve the full co-operation of the West. This does not, and must not, mean that we treat suspicion of that religion *as a religion* as automatically unreasonable.

The left tries to disguise the genuine dangers in Islamic doctrine behind moral equivalency. *What about Christianity and Judaism? Don't they have barbaric ideas?* And sure, there are parts of the holy books of practically every religion that would offend our modern enlightenment-era sensibilities. But there are also centuries of theology that have been written since those holy books that have rendered the offending passages inoperable in the minds of all but the most fanatical believers. Some of these believers are obviously dangerous in their own right — for example, the largely Christian governments of Uganda and Nigeria are difficult to distinguish from Islamic ones in terms of brutality — but globally, they are obvious exceptions. The rest of their faiths have made peace with the enlightenment, and with the ideas that make modern life possible.

Islam has not had its enlightenment.

We keep hearing about reform, we keep hearing about #notallmuslims, about how so many oppose violence. But where are they? Where are the marches on the streets against terrorism by Muslims? They don't exist and I don't think they'll never happen.

The reason is pretty simple: in my experience, there are three types of Muslims. First, there's the Muslim who was born to a Muslim family and knows nothing of Islam but knows their family identity and is generally reflexively defensive of that identity, regardless of the bad behavior of others who bear it. Call these people the "cultural

Muslims."

The second group are the true-believing fanatics, and they're almost always fanatics. These people would never question Allah, or his faith, and generally regard any insult against their religion as cause for violence. At their most extreme, these people turn into sleeper agents for ISIS. Even at less extreme levels, they will riot or assault people who don't conform to their religion's standards. Call these the "zealous Muslims."

Then there are the third group: call them the Scholars. These people genuinely seek reform, are critical of certain interpretations of their religion, and generally want to coexist with the West. In fact, some of them see ways that the traditional values of a peaceful, moderate Islam might curb some of the excesses of leftist cultural domination.

I've met all three groups, and I suspect I'm like most Westerners in that I much prefer the scholars. But kind of like well-adjusted libertarians who aren't on the autism spectrum (and yes, those do exist), these people are vanishingly rare. And because numbers dictate influence, that makes this group almost entirely insignificant to any serious debate about the impacts of Islam on the West. It's not that I'm not grateful that they exist. Frankly, I'd like to see the West encourage and welcome as many of them as possible. I'm just pointing out that they're the exception, and policies based on exceptions are usually bad policies.

So we must address the cultural Muslims and the zealous Muslims. The cultural Muslims won't attack their own religion, and because of that, they won't look for reform. They probably won't be blowing up buildings, but they'll become get defensive, unhelpful, and try to fudge the obvious when someone of their faith does just that. Furthermore, the purely cultural Muslim is as much a minority globally as the scholar. There's slightly more of them, but they're still not the ones driving the bus.

That title belongs to the zealous Muslims, and boy are there a lot of them. They're the people cheering in the streets and chanting Allahu Ackbar during 9/11, regardless of the fact that they were citizens of the same country as the thousands dead.

They're the Muslims in Chicago chanting, "Free Palestine, death to Israel, death to America."

They're the Muslims chanting, "Allahu Akbar" and "Heil Hitler" in the streets of Germany.

They may not actively murder teenagers at a concert, behead a priest or shoot up a magazine office. But they'll certainly provide the weapons and a home for you to hide in. Why do you think it took so long to find the Belgium train station bombers in the Muslim-majority town of Molenbeek? These terrorists have plenty of friends among the alleged "peaceful Muslim majority," almost all of whom are zealous Muslims.

And no, incidents like the Belgian train bombing are not just "isolated incidents." Videos pop up every day on the internet displaying radicals that have planted seeds and communities in the West, and who gloat loudly about it to anyone who'll listen.

We should be listening, but unfortunately, every time these videos pop up, they are drowned out by the mainstream media like clockwork. Muslim men are screaming death to Europe in their mosques? Ignore that! Did you hear about the Southern Poverty Law labeling a cartoon frog a symbol of hate? Did you take the BuzzFeed quiz on which Disney princess you are?[32] Have you seen the Sky News segment on whether you should dress your dog up for Halloween?[33]

And if by some chance these videos do make it to the mainstream, and usually it's only the ones where people end up dead, you immediately hear cries of, "What about Christian terrorism?!" "What about the Crusades!" "Christians were mean to Muslims, too!" "Don't we kinda sorta deserve it as payback for that?"

Firstly, even if I did accept that the Crusades were historically evil, cruelty in the 12th century is not a blank check for equivalent cruelty in the 21st. That was a much more brutal time, whereas these days, running over dozens of parents and their children in your truck is recognized by everyone in the West as an atrocity. Apply modern standards to modern crimes, and maybe get back to that old childhood lesson that two wrongs don't make a right.

But you know what, okay. You want to talk about the Crusades? Let's dance.

The Crusades had nothing to do with Christian extremism or imperialism. The opposite is true. The Crusades happened in part because the Caliphate of the time was viciously and relentlessly

---

32 Yes, and I'm Elsa. Though I somehow doubt my reason for being happy about this — that she claps predatory trading partners in chains and ships them back to their countries like cattle — is what the quiz intended.
33 Please don't. Canine cultural appropriation is not okay.

persecuting Christians who lived in the areas now thought of as Israel and Palestine.[34] And no, not vicious in the way leftists who complain about Bibi Netanyahu use the word. I'm talking about open endorsement of raiding, enslavement, rape, murder, and conquest for roughly 500 years. And that's not even touching on the depredations of the Islamic Caliphate toward Europe, which included sea raids destroying trade and transportation routes (hey, what happened to the love of free trade?), human trafficking of Europeans through the slave trade, burning of churches, raping of nuns, and a state of constant fear over the prospect of Islamic conquest.

In reaction to this obvious and brutal overreach by the dominant caliphate — which doesn't sound familiar at all, does it? — the Crusades took place. Like sword-wielding versions of Twisted Sister, Christendom declared "We're not gonna take it anymore." The people who joined the Crusades gave up their lives to regain their lands, families, and pride. They sold everything they owned in order to buy weapons. They watched as their friends, families, and thousands of fellow Europeans died defending Christianity, warts and all, from its rapacious Islamic rivals.

The Crusaders did absolutely *nothing* wrong. The religious tradition they were defending would ultimately be responsible for everything from the creation of higher learning in the West, to the Protestant work ethic that powered capitalism's rise, to the Enlightenment, and yes, even to the development of universalist ideas that many of today's leftists still believe in without realizing their origins. And we have

---

34 Douthat, Ross. "The Case Against the Case Against the Crusades." New York Times. http://douthat.blogs.nytimes.com/2015/02/10/the-case-against-the-case-against-the-crusades/?_r=0

paid back the people who fought for this tradition by pissing on their graves, and then importing the very Caliphate they defeated through blood, sweat, and tears, and excusing many of the same atrocities they committed then out of fear of "Islamophobia." It's disgusting, sad, and pathetic.

Islam's ambition has been the destruction of Christendom — which is to say, not just Christians, but Jews, European Pagans, and everyone else living under the banner of Western culture — since Muhammad dreamed it up between child brides. The Crusades were a warning of what would be necessary when a Caliphate pushed that ambition too far, as they are presently doing, and will keep doing unless we take similar steps to stop them once and for all. We have been fighting Islam for 1,400 years. To think we can stop that war with Obama-esque apologies and cringing retreat is naïve. Let he who desires peace prepare for war, and let he who desires religious tolerance between the West and Islam prepare for more crusades.

So while leftists attack the Crusaders as evil imperialists, I'm going to be something very different. I'm going to be hoisting the flag and saying "Deus Vult."

Too bad I can't expect most of my fellow young people to join me yet.

6

HOW I RUINED EVERYTHING

So by now, most young people reading this have probably concluded that the West was screwed before they were even born into it. Older readers, meanwhile, must be feeling awfully resentful: "Sure, we made our share of mistakes," they're thinking, "but have you seen what the young people today are doing? Stop shifting blame and whining like the rest of the millennials, Lauren! You guys are making it worse!"

Listen, old folks, I totally hear you, and if you think I've got any illusions that my generation are angels, boy, have you got another thing coming. I know how bad my generation can be, and to prove it, here: I'll tell you a story.

One of the more surreal experiences I consistently go through when I attend left-wing protests is that sometimes people try to get the police to make me go away. One young lady at one particular protest did this in a highly amusing way. Like so many others, she asked the police to remove me. My offense? Saying I didn't believe in white privilege. Yes, according to these people, simply saying that was grounds to remove me from a public place that my tax dollars pay to maintain.

Naturally, the police refused, on the grounds that I was, in fact, free to be in a public place. My accuser responded — with genuine notes of betrayal in her voice — "You're supposed to protect us."

Protect her from what? What harm was I visiting upon her? This is where it got good, as her voice rose into an eventual hectoring shriek:

"Look at all the people who are crying! I shouldn't even be the one saying this; I have privilege! This is F—KED UP! I SHOULDN'T BE SAYING THIS!"

Well, she got the last part right. But look at the first part. Really look at it. My being at a public protest made people *cry* because they couldn't handle even the *presence* of disagreement. Calling that stupidity is an insult to stupid people: sure, they're bad at being rational, but at least they try. There wasn't even the semblance of reason at that protest. The philosopher Alasdair MacIntyre has denounced something called "emotivism," or the idea that morality is only an expression of emotion[35]. I don't believe that all morals are based on emotion, but *these* peoples' morals definitely were. In fact, SJWs in general are to emotivism what Walter White was to crystal meth: manufacturers of its purest, most dangerous form.

There is a good reason for this. SJWs simply would not exist if not for our society twisting natural, human emotional urges — particularly among women — into political mandates. I learned this when I was lucky enough to interview the psychologist Jordan B. Peterson, and PhD student Christine Brophy, late in 2016.[36] Peterson and Brophy

---

35 For more, see MacIntyre, Alasdair. After Virtue. Notre Dame, IN: Notre Dame Press. 2007.
36 Rebel Media. "Where do SJWs Come From?" https://www.youtube.com/watch?v=x_fBYROA7Hk. Accessed

explained that today's SJWs fall into two, mutually reinforcing and equally toxic camps: PC Authoritarians and PC Egalitarians.

The authoritarians' psychological makeup was depressingly familiar and almost entirely toxic. According to Peterson and Brophy, the authoritarians are marked by low verbal intelligence (in other words, they're too stupid to understand subtlety, nuance, or ambiguity in language), by heightened disgust responses of the kind usually associated with crusaders for moral purity, and by emotional disorders like anxiety, depression, or OCD that are usually set off by lack of such purity. In other words, all those people claiming to be "triggered" aren't lying: they really are rather like overanxious, emotional children with similarly childlike understandings of language and morality. This much can probably be chalked up to the helicopter-style of parenting so many millennials experienced, and to the emasculatory, self-esteem -based public-education system they came up through. For all the sneers among SJWs about things like fragile masculinity, or white fragility, in other words, there really is a large chunk of them who came into the world too fragile to function.

But the PC egalitarians were different, and they were the ones who showed where good natural urges can be perverted. Peterson and Brophy told me that PC egalitarians, unlike their authoritarian counterparts, showed high verbal intelligence (they were very good at seeing nuance or complexity), and extremely high levels of empathy: both traits that normally are considered desirable.[37] Basically, they

---

Oct. 31, 2016.

37 Sorry R9K, but not everyone can belong to the sociopathic autist Master Race. We need Chads and Staceys for something.

have the same psychological makeup as extremely smart, nurturing mothers.

The problem, though, was that while they possessed high verbal intelligence and high empathy, what they lacked was judgment in how to apply them. According to Peterson and Brophy, most PC egalitarians had met and cared for people who had experienced some form of "oppression." Therefore, they had come to view those people rather like a mother views her children: uncritically, with a willful incapacity to believe they could do anything wrong. This led them to treat the aforementioned emotionally childlike PC authoritarians (whose constant shrieks of victimization made them appear to suffer pain) like constantly aggrieved toddlers. Which, in practice, means constantly finding rationalizations (using the egalitarians' high verbal intelligence) for the authoritarians' behavior and demands, excusing anything they do wrong, and instinctually and viciously attacking anyone who would harm them.

In short, left-wing politics had taken people whose natural calling was to be mothers (and probably very good ones at that), and turned them into surrogate parents/defenders of the most dysfunctional, broken adult populations, rather than of actual kids. This is what happens when a society treats motherhood like a curse to be avoided, but at the same time treats grown adults like perpetually abused children: the instinct to care for someone more vulnerable and dear to you gets badly confused and twisted.

This gets to a deeper point: even outside Social Justice Warriors, the millennial generation is to humans what French bulldogs are to dogs:

bred to be useless, almost incapable of procreation, and possessed of comically big heads. We are bred to be useless because we have either failed, or haven't been taught, to engage with the most important parts of the human experience at anything more than a shallow level. We are incapable of procreation, because one of the things we're worst at understanding is sex. And as for our big heads? Well, somehow despite being almost completely ignorant, our minds have added insult to injury by not only continuing to form opinions, but being prouder of them the more moronic they are.

For starters, millennials are perhaps uniquely bad at thinking about what institutions or structural forces are required to maintain a free society.

Consider the issue of free speech. Most people obviously find the words of those with whom they passionately disagree to be annoying, or contemptible. Some even find those words dangerous, because they feel threatened by the prospect of the people who speak them attaining power. In some cases, as with communist infiltrators during the Red Scare in Hollywood, or with modern day Western apologists for ISIS, there's good reason to be afraid of some people's ideas, and their expression of them. However, say this for the Red Scare communists: even if their reasons for doing so were inherently self-serving and disingenuous, they did at least defend free speech as a root institution of the West.

Indeed, throughout history, I'm sorry to say that until very recently, the left was better on the question of free speech than the right, even if its actual motives were still obviously vicious. Liberals and leftists of the past understood that suppressing words doesn't actually solve problems, and may actually make those problems worse. For example, one very obvious point is that suppressing words doesn't make the ideas those words represent go away. It just makes the people who hold those ideas harder to spot, because they go underground, or keep quiet publicly. Some may even be radicalized and come to hold more extreme versions of those ideas – ideas that they see no reason not to act on in equally extreme ways, since the words will get them in trouble anyway. This is actually quite likely, due to a psychological phenomenon called reactance, which makes people immediately want to do anything they're told not to do in the most lurid way possible.

In short, free speech is often a way for extremists to identify themselves to the rest of society, and also a good release valve for hard-wired psychological impulses that otherwise might lead to violence. Acknowledging this does not require you to be a right-winger: it just requires you to be someone who wants to avoid massive violence and civil unrest.

Oh wait, sorry, SJWs want those things, apparently. I could point out that they usually lead to extremely reactionary, authoritarian governments, which don't usually favor the left. However, given that the SJW's political theory is basically that they can win by being more reactionary and authoritarian than the right itself, I don't think that'll work. So maybe they'll find this more persuasive:

Let's say you think racism, sexism, homophobia, transphobia, etc, are evil and want to drive them out of polite society. If that's so, I invite you to consider what happens when particularly evil ideas go underground for protracted periods of time. Well, the people who used to know how to defeat those ideas get lazy. They just accept as written that the ideas are wrong, and don't do the hard work necessary to figure out why. This makes the eventual resurgence of those ideas much easier, since they come back against a weaker, more intellectually lazy population.

And don't take my word for it. If you're an SJW, the rise of Trump and the alt right must've been horribly traumatic because you genuinely believed you'd buried the sort of ideas they appeal to. If you believe Trump is secretly a neoconfederate, then how do you expect to beat him, when you don't even know what the confederate case for slavery *was?* If you believe Trump's secretly Hitler 2.0, then how are you going to beat him without knowing something about what was in *Mein Kampf?* You're not, and that leaves you with only shame as a weapon: shame that won't work once it becomes clear that you're using it as a substitute for argument.

Again, if you're trying to create a world that's not congenial to ideas that really deserve to die, whatever those are, then you need free speech in order to know what form those ideas are taking. I'm extremely glad that I can google "Karl Marx" or "the Quran" and find public domain copies of both, and pages upon pages of work from their defenders, because that helps me arm myself in the battle of ideas.

Do millennial SJWs even know to ask these questions? Of course not. They never stop to think what effect so-called "hate speech" laws might have on society, or how they could be easily turned against the very people who created them (I mean, #KillAllMen and #DieCisScum aren't exactly going to pass muster with a judge). For them, the analysis never gets beyond "this thing hurts my feelings and it must be stopped NOW NOW NOW NOW NOW."

The same thing goes especially for sex, which millennials (particularly millennial feminists) seem to want to be both as hedonistic as possible, and as tightly regulated/safe/low-risk as possible. Having basically beaten social conservatives into a fetal position[38] on abortion and contraception, both of which remove the obvious consequences of sex in more or less drastic ways, the new millennial feminist movement is now trying to get rid of even the most minor side-effects of sex: like regretting it after the fact, or forming emotional attachments.

What else can we make of the Kafkaesque "affirmative consent" laws that have sprouted on college campuses, which permit accusations of rape to flower in pretty much any circumstance a woman wants? And what else are we to make of the manner in which millennial feminists loudly trumpet the sluttiest, cattiest parts of hookup culture as empowering precisely because they prevent them ever having to acknowledge a guy (or in their parlance, "f—kboy") having once used him as a human dildo? Answer: millennial feminists want to amputate something that is just a part of human nature — the fact that sex makes women more vulnerable, both emotionally and physically, than men. They want to be entitled to sex that they never regret, or even have to think about, for any reason, and if they have to trample

---

38 Pun intended.

the rights or feelings of the opposite sex into the dust? Hey, turn up the Beyonce. "Who run the world? GIRLS!"

Then they act surprised when men withdraw[39], or revolt[40] against them. Because again, the actual system of sexual politics they're creating never crosses their mind. It's all about getting what they want NOW NOW NOW. And again, the people supporting this aren't shy. They write think pieces. So many. Stupid. Think pieces.

So that's politics and sex, and really, you don't want to get me started on religion or art. Otherwise we'll be talking about the ludicrous argument made by some people my age that Jesus/Muhammad (!) was a feminist, or explaining the numerous ways in which film/music/video game/art criticism among millennials has degenerated into "spot the black person/woman/gay," while artistic merit lies abandoned by the wayside. Well, that or I'll start going off on a tangent about how people have actually translated Shakespeare plays into text message form, complete with misspellings and Emojis. To quote the Bard's own Richard III, "oh monstrous fault, to harbor such a thought!"

At the risk of losing my young person card, if this is the future we're creating, I'm fine with restricting the right to vote to people over 50 and letting the Boomers get another crack at screwing everything up. Because quite frankly, while they may have started the fire, they've only thrown gasoline on it so far. Millennials have turned that into *napalm*.

---

39 Yiannopoulos, Milo. "The Sexodus, Part 1: The Men Giving Up On Women and Checking Out of Society." http://www.breitbart.com/london/2014/12/04/the-sexodus-part-1-the-men-giving-up-on-women-and-checking-out-of-society/. Accessed Oct. 31, 2016.
40 Just google "Men's Rights" or "Gamergate" for this one.

Sorry SJWs, but I don't want to watch the great traditions of Athens, Jerusalem, and Europe consumed in your bonfire of the inanities. Sorry millennial hipsters, but I don't want to see art defined by how many colors the artists are, rather than the colors on the canvas. And, sorry feminists, but I don't want to run the world because of my vagina.

I want to run it because of my ideas: something maybe a fraction of a percent of people my age seem to care about.

Now let's talk about what some of those ideas are.

7

HOW TO STOP RUINING EVERYTHING

Here's a riddle for you: what's the difference between globalism and communism?

One is a discredited utopian ideology pushed by Ivory Tower academics and the left-wing elite, which has wrecked the Third World, attacked Western culture and institutions, devastated the economic health of every nation that's tried it, aspires to one world government, and can't work in a world where some nations reject it. The other fell in the 90s.

The West is withering away from cancer, and globalism is the cancer. There is no iteration of globalism that can service the needs of free peoples. Left-wing globalism is simply Communism Lite, where a Marxist culture replaces a Marxist economy. Right-wing globalism is an intermediate step to left-wing globalism that hates white people for being lazy rather than oppressive, treats religious people as useful idiot missionaries rather than backwards un-people, worships corporations instead of international government, and rationalizes political correctness with the language of a corporate HR department instead of the language of a Marxist faculty lounge.

Let's review what we know so far.

We know that globalism is the product of the psychology of the Baby Boomers: a spoiled, naïve, hardship-averse generation who treat only the Coca Cola "I'd like to teach the world to sing in perfect harmony" commercial as revealed truth. The Boomer left is trapped in a fantasy of the glory days where they could wax rhapsodic about fighting the system and saving the world from war, all while they prop up a system that expropriates the incomes of millennials and gives it back to Boomers as entitlements. The Boomer right is equally trapped in a fantasy of the glory days where they could pretend to bestride the world like a colossus from junior staffer positions in the Bush administration(s), where we never run out of taxes to cut, or of younger, poorer people to kill in the wars they start, and where they can execute a hypocrisy-free pivot from sexual hedonism to neo-Victorian moralizing the instant people stop wanting to sleep with them.

We know that globalism is built on the twin pillars of imported cheap labor and exported jobs, which boost the Third World at the expense of the First, treat increased crime as an acceptable cost for increased GDP, and which transform self-reliant nations of builders into cringing nations of servants.

We know that for globalists, the only important thing about a global caliphate is that it has the word "global" in the name. So long as iPhones are cheap, they don't care if future generations must live under the effective yoke of blasphemy laws, anti-gay ordinances, or the stifling, small world of a burqa and hijab. Hell, why should the Boomers care? Those damn kids are too sexually liberated and offensive anyway!

We know that those kids aren't alright. In fact, they're acquiescing in their own dispossession: dispossession of their political rights, their economic condition, their capacity to create the next generation, and most of all, their culture. They're doing this because the education system and the forces of political correctness are making their world smaller and sadder by the day, cutting them off from every inch of their heritage and nature that might rebel against indoctrination. We know the future, if left to the hands of the average millennial, is an Ugg boot stomping on a human face, forever.[41]

Most of all, we know we have to fix this, or watch the West light itself up like a Roman candle, then forget what Rome was and fling open its gates to the Vandals to avoid being called racist. But how do we fix it? What does the better world look like? That's the question I mean to answer now.

It all starts with nationalism.

There's a reason every self-help book starts with self-love. You can't move on with your life unless you love yourself. You can't begin to date or help others until you've helped yourself. It's decent and lovely to want to save the world, but you certainly can't do it on your death bed.

And the West is on its death bed. It can't take much more. It's given

---

41 Still glad I finally read 1984.

up so much of what has made it healthy for the sake of appeasing others. Watching what globalism, immigration and Islam has done to the West is like watching a woman in an abusive relationship who can't stop making excuses for the man who hits her. Like it or not, both establishment liberals and even most establishment "conservatives" have become the battered wives of the barbarians.

Everyone is in denial. They are utterly delusional.

Nationalism is a hard sell for many people. Millennials in particular have an almost Pavlovian anxious reaction to the word nationalism. Their minds conjure images of red flags adorned with spidery black symbols, of hands raised at 45-degree angles, and of words shrieked from underneath a stupid little mustache. In short, we hear nationalism and assume that the person pushing it is Literally Hitler™.

Well, guess what? I'm not Hitler, figuratively or literally. As far as I'm concerned, Hitler was just a SJW who happened to get freaky amounts of power and actually implement his #KillAllJews (the predecessor to #KillAllMen) worldview. Basically, if Hitler were writing today, he could've avoided all the verbiage in *Mein Kampf* and just complained about "Jew-splaining" on Tumblr and the message would be the same.

Oh, and another problem I have with Hitler? He fawned over Muslims more sycophantically than Justin Trudeau. Bibi Netanyahu was right to point out that Hitler decided on the Holocaust partly because Middle Eastern Muslims told him they didn't want Jews expelled into the region.[42] That's some commitment to showing how much you're not an Islamophobe. And to give little Adolf his due, he wasn't: he was actually more of an Islamophile, truth be told. He even wished he was Muslim himself.[43] Yes, that's right: on top of being a whiny art student who scapegoated an allegedly "privileged" race for all his problems, and talked a bunch of violent, angry people into siding with him (like any good SJW), Hitler also wished he was Muslim. He might've been a nationalist by technicality, but he was more in the New Black Panthers style of "nationalist" than the Trump style. Frankly, I think today, he'd be one of those low-T Tumblr crazies who join ISIS and end up on the news.

Oh yeah, and let's not forget: Hitler was a socialist. I'm not. Like most young right-wingers, I've had my libertarian phase, and I still think capitalism is pretty awesome. Like any other ideal, nationalism included, you can't take it so far that you turn into a crazy person. But hey, not every libertarian is a tinfoil hat wearing crank.

Just like every nationalist is not a freaking Hitler clone.

The fact is that nationalism is a great, necessary idea that's gotten a bad rap because a couple of idiots used it to justify their own idiocy, and happened to do it comparatively recently. Everyone likes to complain about Hitler and Mussolini, but everyone forgets that without nationalism, we wouldn't have a Germany or an Italy to get mad at for Hitler and Mussolini. Without nationalism, we'd probably still be

---

42 Haaretz staff. "Netanyahu: Hitler Didn't Want to Exterminate the Jews." Haaretz. http://www.haaretz.com/israel-news/1.681525. Oct. 21, 2015.

43 Green, Dominic. "Why Hitler Wished He Was Muslim." Wall Street Journal. http://www.wsj.com/articles/book-review-ataturk-in-the-nazi-imagination-by-stefan-ihrig-and-islam-and-nazi-germanys-war-by-david-motadel-1421441724. Jan. 16, 2015.

at war with the freaking Habsburg Empire. And without nationalist movements in Poland and other Soviet satellite states, we couldn't have taken the Soviet Union down, either. Nationalism is what builds societies, and yes, just like how millennials take self-esteem too far, folks like Hitler, Mussolini, or Malik Shabazz take nationalism too far.

Oh, and just to make an unpleasant-but-accurate point, the nationalism that Hitler and Mussolini subscribed to owes as much to progressives like Woodrow Wilson (who propagandized national identity near the end of the First World War to fight imperial European powers) as it does to any form of nationalism that preceded it. So along with being as unhealthy as the nationalism of the New Black Panthers, Hitler and Mussolini's nationalism shares one other thing in common with them: it rose out of the machinations of well-meaning but idiotic leftists.

So get that stupid little mustache out of your head. I'm not the Nazi you're looking for, and nationalism is more than just not-that-bad. It's *awesome*. Particularly the kind of pan-Western nationalism I'm talking about here, which actually doesn't have a precedent of either a positive or negative kind in history. It's simply too ambitious. But unlike the utopian fever dream that is globalism, I think this kind of nationalism has a chance at defining world politics for centuries. Why? Because it conforms to human nature. Indeed, once you strip away the examples of people abusing nationalism for the sake of their own mental illness, you eventually realize that its superiority to globalism is actually based on one of the most healthy parts of human nature: the preference for a group that supports each other, like a family.

That's not an idle comparison. Families, in my view, are the first nationalist units. You feed your kids first because you care for them, but also because later on in life they will likely feed you. The support and help you foster among your family will continue on throughout generations. Evolution itself says that we are hard-wired to create families and to pass on our genes, which are our own miniature individual forms of national identity. A globalist form of family would require its members to essentially surrender control of its belongings and food to any other family that needs them. As altruistic and noble as that might seem to the cucks among us, it would be cruel to your own children who need that support. Not only that, your family line — and you with it — would die.

The West needs to think of itself as a family again, not as a sugar daddy for other people and their families. That doesn't mean we have to immediately mistrust all foreigners. With apologies to Bill Buckley, I would sooner be governed by the first thousand legal Mexican immigrants to enter the United States this year than by the lily white staff of the *Huffington Post*. Welcoming people who are culturally Western, or who subscribe to the ideals that make up Western culture, just makes sense, the same way it makes sense for different families to intermarry. But that intermarriage and adoption of people who belong with us needs to be done on our terms. It needs to be done with the understanding that we are accepting people into a family, and that such acceptance is a precious thing that must be earned, not given away. Without this preference for people who belong and who share its ideals, the West will wither and die faster than a flower watered with tequila.

So what do we do to create the new, positive form of nationalism? I'm glad you asked.

Firstly, we need to re-learn that borders are good, necessary things. In America, this process has gotten a great kick from president-elect Donald Trump, whose campaign was able to dominate the Republican Party based mostly on his promise to build a wall and enforce immigration law with the aggressiveness it deserves. Whether we like Trump or not, we have to acknowledge the statesmanship of this pitch.

Trump saw something with greater moral clarity than other politicians: that a nation which tries to sustain potentially endless numbers of illegal immigrants can never tend to its own garden and may some day become the very place people seek to escape. People come here because we have great shares of resources, but resources are not infinite, and a nation with 30 million immigrants whose welfare checks outpace their taxes is a nation whose scarce resources will only get scarcer and scarcer. Yes, it's something of a compliment that so many people want to come to countries like America, just as it's a compliment for the prettiest girl in school to have every man asking her out. But if that girl lets all those guys into her, her body will get used up fast, and the same thing goes for a country. To borrow a line from the feminists, sometimes no means no. The Trump campaign was America's rape whistle.

Not that we have to say no to everyone, or even most people. After all, Trump never foreclosed the possibility of a generous immigration policy. He repeatedly talked about the "big, beautiful door" he wanted to build in his wall. But there's a big difference between throwing the door to your house open and not having the door at all. There is nothing welcoming about a house without a door, because there was never a choice to leave the door open. Similarly, America's present lack of border control robs not just her people, but the immigrants themselves, of a sense of legitimacy. How can immigrants be optimistic or proud of the nation they join, if they know that nation might reject them if it ever gave itself the choice? And how can its people ever really welcome those immigrants if their very presence feels like a predatory exploitation of their own country's weakness, rather than a voluntarily accepted compact between the newcomer and their peers? The answer is, obviously, that immigrants cannot fully assimilate to a country whose acceptance they cannot guarantee, and that country's residents cannot fully accept people to whose presence they never consented. Period. End of story.

So first, we need to build walls, even if only so that we can add doors later.

Secondly, we need to decide just who we *do* actually want to let through those doors. Though perhaps it's easier to decide who we *don't* want. Muslims, especially from the Third World, easily top that list. The left will no doubt whine about religious freedom, but at the point where they have exercised their power globally to undermine every religion that actually built the West, their complaints can be safely ignored. And despite the protestations of cucked religious conservatives more concerned with principle than survival, there is nothing unreasonable or unconservative about the proposals by the likes of Frauke Petry, Marine Le Pen, Viktor Orban, or Donald Trump himself to limit Islamic immigration. Conservatism, once upon a time, stood for prudence. These proposals are entirely prudent.

We do not need theory to prove this. The experience of Europe is guide enough. Despite specious comparisons of anti-Muslim sentiment to anti-Semitic prejudices that gave rise to the Holocaust, the fact is that Islamic immigrants have brought a wave of anti-Semitism down on Europe.[44] Their intolerance extends beyond Jews, however. More than half of British Muslims seek a legal ban on homosexuality.[45] Shariah law courts systematically abuse women everywhere that they exist. A majority of Muslims in almost every country where they live say a wife must obey her husband.[46] One Muslim cleric caught on tape even defended sex with nine year olds because Muhammad did it.[47] Anti-Muslim sentiment makes you a Nazi? No, it makes you someone who wants nothing to do with a people who are Nazis in all but name. It's no accident that Hitler and his SJW heirs love these people. Doesn't mean we have to.

But even once you get past Muslim immigrants, there is another point, which is that immigration policy in the West simply fails to be remotely meritocratic. Immigrants are not let in to fill niches where our countries need help, or to contribute in some way to society. It's even considered controversial in some circles to suggest that immigrants should be able to pull their own weight. All of this must be reversed. In the U.S., a good start would be repealing the

---

44 Barber, Ben. "Muslim Migrants Fan European Anti-Semitism." Huffington Post. http://www.huffingtonpost.com/ben-barber/muslim-migrants-fan-europ_b_9395896.html. March 3, 2016.
45 Greene, Richard and Hume, Tim. "52% of British Muslims in poll think homosexuality should be illegal." CNN. http://www.cnn.com/2016/04/11/europe/britain-muslims-survey/. April 12, 2016.
46 Pew Center. "Chapter 4: Women In Society." Pew Research Center. http://www.pewforum.org/2013/04/30/the-worlds-muslims-religion-politics-society-women-in-society/. April 30, 2013.
47 https://www.youtube.com/watch?v=Lc6GVg3GfuI

Immigration Act of 1965, so that things like national origin can be factored into our calculus, and so that limits on immigration from other Western countries can be removed. Everywhere else, the same sort of measures must be taken.

The Statue of Liberty's base might say "give me your tired, your poor, your huddled masses yearning to breathe free," but fun fact: that inscription wasn't on the original statue. Rather, it was chiseled on at the request of the wealthy New York donors who'd built the pedestal. Which just goes to show that the rich donors from New York haven't been right about immigration in over a century. In the new nationalist world, it may be that we still take the tired and poor. But at the very least, we should only do so *provided* that they also yearn to breathe free, and free in the sense understood historically by Western civilization.

Speaking of meritocracy, our society needs to get back to that, too, particularly in the battle of ideas. So the third thing we have to do in order to bring about a renewed, positive nationalism is to restore a fair battle of ideas. The only way to ensure this is to ensure that complete free speech and expression triumph, and that those that try to destroy either are denied the power.

Today, censorship proceeds not primarily from the government, but from the power of social sanction from a dominant culture ruled by the corporate and media left. Those of us on the right need to rediscover the capacity to argue against private censorship and the usage of corporate power to stifle dissent: absolute corporate *laissez faire* will simply lead to us being treated as court jesters. Too much is at stake to let masturbatory displays of philosophical purity hijack our cause. Yes, the left tried to destroy institutions with some of the same ideas, but that's simply proof that to restore Western civilization, we need to build institutions that can withstand those kinds of assaults. A free marketplace of ideas enables us to consider all options to do that.

Fourthly, and perhaps most crucially, entitlement culture must be destroyed. In the 60s, the U.K. and America had a culture that would leave one ashamed to be on the dole, to not have a job. So great was this stigma that up until the mid-60s, even liberal Democrats saw it as their goal to get Americans off the dole, and would have succeeded if not for over-perfectionism and white guilt getting in the way.[48] JFK himself put this bygone attitude famously as "ask not what your country can do for you, but what you can do for your country."

In a world like this, where people actively pushed against the shame of welfare, a welfare state can work as it was intended: as a safety net for those temporarily on hard times. Only when people treat welfare as an ugly necessity for the temporarily humbled, or for defeated, failed human beings with nowhere else to go, can it avoid becoming a machine for the creation of mass-entitlement.

Needless to say, we don't live in a world where welfare recipients are the sorts of people who only need a quick hand up and will go back to work immediately after a shower and a new suit. Indeed, I don't think anyone really *wants* to succeed anymore, period. They want to do as little as possible. They want to fly under the radar for fear of being disagreeable. They want to cheat the system and are

---

48 For more on this, see Murray, Charles. Losing Ground. New York: Basic Books. 1984.

happy to brag about it. And all the while, our welfare systems and the culture of entitlement that supports them, grows until it consumes everything that sustains it. To solve this, curtailing the welfare state is obviously important. But more important is a cultural revival of the idea that failure should be a source of shame, that losers should be shunned and even mocked, and that compassion unmotivated by justice is simply enabling in a pretty package.

Concomitant with this is a different idea that must also experience a revival: the idea that success through the power of the human will represents humanity at its best. This idea has formed the soul of the West for centuries, yet now it is under attack. Self-fulfilling prophecies of cynicism have replaced the classical ideas that you can achieve anything you want if you work hard; that every man, no matter what his skin color or class, can beat the next through pure power of will; that all our wildest dreams of flying in the sky, mastering the sea and even going to space can be achieved. The young Americans who once had sparkles in their eyes and dreams of a better future now have only resentment, envy, and blame for others. It's time we told the people who taught them this nonsense that no, it's not that no one can beat the odds and the privileges of others: it's just that you're too *weak*.

This is hard stuff to swallow, and frankly, I fear it won't be accepted unless the West suffers even more from its abandonment of these sorts of principles. But 2016 showed us that such feelings of pride in the face of despair are already starting to surface. Donald Trump's rise to the Presidency was fueled by people who had otherwise decided to give up on justice or merit ever triumphing in our broken, decadent society. Meanwhile, the apostles of that brokenness and decadence, whether they came from Wall Street, Hollywood, or Martha's Vineyard, worshiped at the altar of Clintonian degeneracy. In fairness, it's easy for them to do when their gated communities, private bodyguards, and country clubs will always keep them at arm's length from the hordes of uneducated fanatics and criminals that they would willingly invite.

But as Trump's triumph shows, they will need every inch of that arm's length to stay safe and fat soon. For even absent the refugees and human garbage they seek to import, so many frustrated members of the younger generations are waking up. They are realizing that our elites are a wet blanket thrown over the torch of Western civilization. Our remedy for that situation will not be gentle.

Those of us who have seen this truth are ready and prepared to fight. Not least of all because we are young, and we will inherit this world long after the tenured communists, the entitled pensioners, and the self-appointed guardians of respectability that make up the Baby Boom generation finally meet the grave. We know we will have to deal with the debts they racked up in order to keep their cushy pensions, the crime and social unrest they invited in order to have someone cut the grass on the cheap, and the attack on our very way of life that they welcomed in order to pointlessly signal their own virtue.

We have to watch as our cultures abandon an ocean of freedoms for tiny islands of licensed deviance. We have to watch as the flags in our windows change from German to Turkish, or from American to Mexican. We have to watch as our streets become Hobbesian war zones, as our native English is treated as a dying language, and as patriotism is mocked. We have to watch as our paychecks are sucked dry to pay for pensions built for richer people, health care built for lazier people, education built for stupider people, and kindness to unworthy people.

We are the people who will be forced to wake up to the failure of multiculturalism, liberalism, and globalism. And the alarm is ringing ever louder in our ears.

The façade of globalist hegemony is going to crumble. Its enablers in the modern media are already dying at the hands of the Internet and the alternative right-wing media that has risen from it like a phoenix. Without a capacity to control the information that their constituents see, globalist politicians will see their racket upended as surely as the Soviet Union was brought down.

I say "right-wing" media will beat this, because frankly, it's time to retire the term "conservative" to describe the right. My generation sees nothing worth conserving in the modern world. And we shouldn't. To be a literal conservative today is to tacitly support the left. To be on the right today is to want to restore things that have been lost: things like merit, justice, virtue, and nationhood.

But we have not lost truth, and with truth, all other things can be found. The right-wingers already rising in my generation and those that come after us will make sure of that.

With apologies to the band Genesis, the West today is a land of confusion. There are too many people making too many problems, and not much truth to go around.

But if we come home to our Western values, I am confident that my generation will, indeed, put it right.

ABOUT THE AUTHOR

Lauren Southern is a right-wing activist, writer and pundit for TheRebel.media. She is well known for her commentary on feminism, free speech, and immigration. Lauren has contributed to a number of programs and websites including CBC radio, BBC Radio, The Libertarian Republic, Spiked Online, IB Times, and Sky News. She is an avid reader and lover of liberty, individualism, and responsibility.

ABOUT THEREBEL.MEDIA

TheRebel.media is a leading independent source of news, opinion and activism. Launched by Ezra Levant and a group of dedicated Rebels after The Sun News Network shutdown. The Rebel is essential for anyone looking for "the other side of the story" in Conservative news in Canada and across the world. www.therebel.media

Made in the USA
Columbia, SC
22 January 2018